Dedicated to the memory of Jo Spier, 1900-1978: Friend, Father and Teacher.

The Legend of
NEW AMSTERDAM

The Legend of
NEW AMSTERDAM

Written and Illustrated by Peter Spier

Doubleday & Company, Inc., Garden City, New York

Library of Congress Catalog Card Number 78-6032   ISBN 0-385-13179-8
Trade 0-385-13180-1   Prebound   Illustrations and text copyright
© 1979 by Peter Spier   All Rights Reserved   Printed in the United States of America   First Edition

You would have called it a village, but the people who lived here, and had built every bit of it with their own hands, grandly called it "de Stad": The City.

It had been founded in the wilderness only thirty-five years before by a handful of families who had been dropped off in a strange land by four small Dutch ships.

Funny names those ships had: COW, HORSE, SHEEP, and MACKEREL. Well-named, too, for besides the people, they had carried the first three animals in their holds. Maybe MACKEREL should have been christened PIG, for those were on board as well.

In the first years the newcomers lived like moles in shallow pits roofed over with tree trunks and branches, covered with dirt.

But in 1660, New Amsterdam was quite a town with its three hundred buildings, and nearly fifteen hundred people!

And still growing.

It was a bustling, cheerful place, where men and women worked hard. And their children worked as well: in Meester Roelantsen's Trivial School in the morning (tuition: two beaver skins per child per year!), and after school at home, feeding the animals, cleaning stables, and weeding gardens.

But once those chores had been done, children's days really began, for there was more to be seen and more to be done in New Amsterdam than you'd believe possible.

First of all there was the gristmill, worked by Jacob Kip, covered with flour dust, white as a ghost.

Nearby, within Fort Amsterdam, were the Church of Saint Nicholas, the Company soldiers, and on the ramparts, the great guns, each with a neat stack of shot beside it.

Across from the Market Field was the town: homes, taverns, offices, shops, and the New Hospital.

More? But of course: there was the Weighing House with its enormous scales and iron weights, and its busy pier where the ferries to Breuckelen and the islands tied up.

There was the sawmill, where huge logs were cut into beams and planks by blades with vicious teeth like a shark's. A scary, dusty place, that sawmill.

There were the shipyard, the ropewalk, the breweries, and the warehouses, some filled with mountains of stinking otter and beaver pelts, or with bundles of tobacco leaves, or stacked barrels.

It was always amazing to watch Evert Duyckingh blow glass bottles, or to hang around Jorissen's smithy for a while, and see the sparks fly off the anvil like shooting stars.

Hendrick Spiers would forever be making something new in his carpenter's shop, and in summer the Company gardens and the farms beyond the wall were worth the trip.

In the bay there were merchantmen riding at anchor, and at times a visiting warship, bristling with cannon and men.

In the street you'd always meet people you knew. Sometimes even the Director General of the Colony of New Netherland himself, the Honorable, Noble Pieter Stuyvesant, appeared, looking stern and haughty, stomping along on his silver-studded wooden leg. Behind his back they jeered, "...he acts as if he is the Czar of Muscovy!" and called him "Peg-Leg Piet."

It was a wonderful town!

Saturday was Market Day, a very special day. The field was crowded with townspeople, farmers, cattle, booths, and visiting Indians.

Even better was the "Kermis" in the fall, the annual Fair, with a merry-go-round, games, stalls, music, and boat races—and no school that day!

Then it would soon be the Feast of Sinterklaas, Saint Nicholas, with Christmas just around the corner, and New Year's Eve, when the soldiers in the fort and the ships in the bay all would fire their guns.

Still, there was one thing and one thing only, that was more fun than anything else, and that was teasing Crazy Annie.

Her real name was Annetje Jans Bogardus, a widow who lived in a small, run-down house surrounded by a neglected garden, close to the water's edge.

Her husband had been killed by the Indians in 1651, and ever since that dreadful day she had not been the same.

The Honorable West India Company paid her a small pension. Kindly neighbors saw to it that she got enough to eat and had plenty of firewood in winter, and they cared for her when she was ill.

She was rather frightening to look at, with her unkempt hair and tattered, worn-out clothes.

Children followed her wherever she went, shouting, "Witch! Witch! Witch!" or repeating over and over again in something vaguely resembling a melody, "Cra-zy An-nie, Cra-zy An-nie!"

Yet the old woman, perfectly harmless, would hardly take notice of them.

Grown-ups would stop the children, of course, whenever they could, saying, "Go home! Leave Annie alone!"

But five minutes later they would be at it again.

There was more to it than that, though, for whenever you would come upon Annetje Jans she would be staring up at the sky, no matter whether it was clear or cloudy, rain or shine. Then she would shake her head in silence, and shuffle off with that strange limping gait of hers, only to stand still again a bit farther on, staring up in another direction.

When someone would ask, not unkindly, "Say, Annetje, what are you looking at? What do you see up there?" she would start cackling with laughter and whisper, "...people and

stone... people and stone..." Then, louder and louder, she would repeat with great insistence, "People and stone! PEOPLE AND STONE!" pointing a skinny arm at the empty sky and cry, "Look! Can't you see? People and stone!"

Most would shake their heads a little sadly, a few might chuckle, and someone would usually take her arm and see her safely home.

Annetje would keep on mumbling, "...people and stone..."

But the children thought the whole thing sidesplitting, a hilarious treat! The funniest, most entertaining show in the whole world!

So whenever they ran into old Annetje and asked, "Hey, Crazy Annie, what do you see?" holding their breath in anticipation, the poor demented woman would immediately look into the air, and pointing to heaven, repeat at the top of her voice, "People and stone...believe me. Just look! PEOPLE AND STONE!"

It was an everlasting amusement for the children, who never tired of their cruel game.

It went so far that even Dominee Drisius had to admonish them sternly in Sunday school, and later that morning mentioned it to their parents before his sermon!

But for the children of New Amsterdam the temptation proved just too great, and they kept on pestering Crazy Annie, even after their mothers had told them a hundred times to leave her alone, and after some fathers had handed out a hard, well-deserved spanking.

Annetje Jans grew more and more feeble, and rarely went outside any longer. Yet whenever she did, children would quickly come running to ask, "What do you see, Annie?" and that, as it always had, would set her off. "Look, up there . . . people and stone . . . Everywhere!"

When she died they buried her next to her husband in the Heere Straet cemetery. Her house was sold, and before long she was almost forgotten. But not quite.

For people talking about someone might say, "...that Cornelis Pluyvier is a nut! He's as crazy as Annie."

It practically became part of the language. "Crazy as Annie." And in that strange way the memory of Annetje Jans Bogardus lived on.

The City grew. Annie's grave was lost, as were those of all the others, Peg-Leg Piet's included, when homes were built on the site of the old graveyard.

New Amsterdam became New York. Breuckelen became Brooklyn. The Heere Straet became Broadway, and the land of old man Bronck became the Bronx. The fort was razed, the mills broken up, the canals filled in. And Dutch was no longer spoken nor understood.

Annetje Jans was forgotten. And yet...

People who had never heard of her, and
could not care less, having been born
generations after she had died, still would say,
"....oh, her [or him!]? She's as crazy as
Annie!" without having the slightest idea who,
or what, Annie had been.

But right they were, for poor old Annetje
had surely been weak in the head. Daft.
Loony. Stark raving mad!

...Or was she?

Description And Key To The Plan

WITHIN FORT AMSTERDAM

1. Dutch Reformed Church of St. Nicholas; 2. Governor's house; 3. barracks for Company soldiers; 4. guardhouse; 5. officers' quarters or storehouse; 6. secretary's office.

a. the gristmill; b. the sawmill; c. cemetery; d. small fortification; e. the Land Gate; f. the Water Gate; g. Weighing House Pier; h. probable site of the gallows.

BLOCK A

1. tavern of Lodewyck Pos: captain of the Rattle Watch; 2. Pieter Laurenzen Cock; 3. Martin Cregier, tavernkeeper and captain of Burger Guard; 4, 5. Jacob de Lang; 6. Dominee Joh. Megapolensis, first Protestant missionary to the Indians; 7. Lucas Andries 8. Barent Cruytdop; 9. Dirck Wiggers; 10. tavern of Lucas Dircksen; 11. Reindert Jansen Hoorn; 12, 13. Dominee Samuel Drisius; 14. Laurens Andriessen; 15, 16. Paulus Leendersen van der Grift, sea captain and trader; 17. Hendrick van Dyck; 18. Jacobus Vis; 19. Cornelis Jansen Pluyvier, innkeeper; 20. Dominee Samuel Drisius; 21. West India Company garden; 22. West India Company's orchard.

BLOCK B

1. Augustine Herrman, artist and merchant; 2. Pieter Schaefbanck, jailer; 3. Joseph Waldron; 4. Resolveert Waldron; 5. Dirck Siecken; 6. Leendert Aerden; 7. Hendrick Hendricksen; 8, 9. Dominee Samuel Drisius; 10. Couwenhoven's brewery; 11. the Latin School.

BLOCK C

1, 2. residence and tavern of Abraham Pietersen; 3. Gerrit Fullewever; 4. Sergeant Pieter Webel; 5. Geertie, widow of Andries Hoppen; 6. Ensign Dirck Smit; 7. Jan Hendricksen van Gunst; 8. Thomas Fransen; 9. Samuel Edsal, owner; Jan Fries, tenant; 10. Weyntje Elbers, widow of Aert Willemsen; 11. Isaac Gravenraet; 12. Peter Rudolphus; 13. Gabriel de Haas; 14. boardinghouse of Claes Ganglofs Visscher; 15. Jacobus Kip; 16. Jacobus Vis; 17, 18. Col. Philip Pietersen Schuyler; 19. Deacon's House for the Poor; 20, 21. Jacobus Kip; 22. Pieter Rudolphus; 23. Jan Cornelissen, Weighing House porter; 24. Jacob Mensen; 25. Daniel Tourneur; 26, 27, 28. Coenraet ten Eyck; 29. Dirck Jansen; 30. Boele Roeloffsen; 31. Thomas Fredericksen; 32. Toussaint Briel; 33, 34, 35, 36. Thomas Wandel; 37. Willem Bredenbent; 38, 39, 40. Egbert Woutersen; 41. Jan Jansen, owner; Christiaen Pieters, tenant.

BLOCK D

1. Frederick Arentsen; 2. Gerrit Hendricksen; 3. Nicolaes Boot; 4. Barentzen family, tenants; Jan Bout, owner; 5. Joh. Verveelen; 6, 7. Oloff Stevensen van Cortlandt. He also owned 14. 8. Pieter van Naarden; 9. Coenraet ten Eyck; 10, 11. Reynout Reynoutsen; 12. Gerrit Jansen Roos; 13. Hendrick Jansen Spiers; 15. Frederick Lubbertsen; 16. Abraham de la Noy; 17, 18. residence and brewery of Oloff Stevensen van Cortlandt, burgomaster 1655–65; 19. Isaac de Forest; 20. offices of Amsterdam firm of Gillis Verbrugge & Co., Dutch traders; 21. Jeronimus Ebbingh; 23. surgeon Varrevanger; 24. Frederick Philipse; 25. Teunis Thomassen; 26. Gerrit Hendricksen.

BLOCK E

1. Hendrick Willems; 2. Frederick van den Bergh, wine and tobacco merchant; 3. Warnaer Wessels, former home of Dominee Bogardus, first permanent clergyman in New Amsterdam; 4. Pieter Jacobsen Buys; 5. Jane, widow of George Holmes, one of the earliest English settlers; 6. office of Jacques Cortelyou, surveyor; 7. Frederick Gijsbertsen van den Bergh; 8. the "five houses" of the W. I. Co. for employees and storage; 9. New Hospital, built 1659–60; 10. W. I. Co. secretary's and sheriff's office; 11. Caspar Steymensen; 12. Jan Jansen; 13. Jacob Kip and Jacob Streycker; 14. Jacob Kip; 15, 16. Isaac Kip; 17. Oloff Stevensen van Cortlandt; 18. Symon Jansen Romeyn; 19, 20. Hendrick Willems; 21, 22. Anthony Jansen van Salee, nicknamed "Anthony the Turk"; 23, 24, 25, 26. Hendrick Hendricksen Kip.

BLOCK F

1. Cornelis van Steenwyck; 2. tavern of Hendrick Jansen Smith; 3. tavern of Hans Dreper; 4, 5. Frans Jansen van Hooghten; 6. bakeshop of Nicolaes Jansen; 7. hatter's shop of Samuel Edsal; 8. Johannes de Decker; 9. Allardt Anthony, one of the first lawyers; 10, 11. "van Tienhoven's Great House," property of his heirs and creditors; 12. warehouse of Augustine Herrmann; 13 warehouse of the West India Co.; 14. van der Grift's warehouse; 15, 16. Cornelis Steenwyck, burgomaster; 17. Dr. Hans Kierstede, the town's first regular physician.

BLOCK G

1. Trijn Jonas, town's first midwife; 2. Annetje Jans Bogardus; 3. Jacob Steendam, New Amsterdam's first poet; 4. Juriaen Blanck; 5. tavern of Michiel Tadens; 6. estate of Joh. van Beeck; 7. Claes Claessen Bordingh; 8. Hendrick Hendricksen Obe, city drummer; 9. Claes Jansen; 10. Isaac Gravenraet; 11. Jacques Cousseau; 12. Pieter van Couwenhoven, brewer.

BLOCK H

1. Jan Dircksen Meyer; 2. Paulus Heymans; 3. James Hubbard, one of the founders of Gravesend, L.I.; 4, 5. Jan Evertsen Bout; 6. Isaac Gravenraet.

BLOCK J

1. Thomas Lambertsen; 2. Pieter Jacobsen Marius; 3. Nicholaes Verlett; 4. Claes Jansen de Ruyter; 5. lot owned by Jacques Cousseau; 6. François Allard; 7, 8. Sara Pietersen, wife of William Thomas Cock; 9. Gillis Pietersen van der Gouw, Paulus Schrick, tenant; 10. Egbert van Borsum, operator of ferry to Breuckelen; 11. Pieter Cornelissen van der Veen; 12. Nicasius de Sille, probably occupied by his son Laurens; 13. Nicholaes Verlett, brother-in-law of Governor Stuyvesant; 14. Pieter Stuyvesant's "Great House"; 15. tavern of Michiel Jansen Vreeland; 16. warehouse of Jacob Stoffelsen.

BLOCK K

1–8. original grant to Dominee Samuel Drisius, who built the four houses on the present Broad Street, and the four facing the Wall; 9. Jan Jansen; 10. Abraham Kermell; 11. Hendrick Jansen Sluyter; 12. Cornelis Hendricksen; 13. Arent Lourens; 14. Janneken Bonus, wife of Thomas Verdon; 15. widow of Albert Jansen.

BLOCK L

1. Douwe Hermsen; 2. Jan Swaen, of Stockholm; 3. Jacob Strycker; 4. Jacob Luybeck; 5. Jacob Strycker and Secretary Cornelis van Ruyven; 6. "Trivial School," elementary Latin school; 7. Thomas Wandel; 8. Nicasius de Sille, Secretary and Sheriff of W.I. Co.'s colony; 9. Augustine Herrman, occupied by Pieter Pietersen, the Mennonite; 10. Red Lion brewery, Isaac de Forest, Joh. Verveelen, and the De la Montagnes, owners; 11. Albert Pietersen.

BLOCK M

1. Robert Roelantsen, Willem Abrahamsen van der Borden, tenant; 2. Pieter Geysen; 3. brewhouse of Michiel Jansen Vreeland; 4. Geertje Jans Stoffels; 5. Meindert Barentsen; 6. Dirck Jansen van Deventer; 7. Thomas Wandel; 8, 9. house and warehouse of Rutger Jacobsen, occupied by Abraham de Lucena, prominent Jewish merchant; 10. Dominee Joh. Megapolensis; 11. Jan Reyndersen; 12. Evert Duyckingh, glassmaker and limner; 13. Joost Goderus; 14. "The House of the Company's Negroes," built by the W.I. Co., before 1643, to house its slaves; 15. tavern of Adriaen Vincent, a Walloon; 16. skipper Thomas Davidts; 17, 18. John Vincent and Anna Vincent, children of Adriaen Vincent; 19, 20. Abraham Jansen; 21. tavern of Jan Rutgersen; 22. Jacobus Backer; 23. Jochem Beeckman.

BLOCK N

1, 2. house and brewery of Jacob Wolphersen van Couwenhoven; 3. Claes Carstensen, a Norwegian; 4. Grietje Dircks, wife of Barent Gerritsen; 5. Magdalena Waele, wife of Gysbert Teunissen; 6. Thomas Wandel; 7. tavern of Pieter Andriessen; 8, 9, 10. Nicholaes de Meyer of Holsteyn; 11. Tielman van Vleck; 12. tavern of Aris Otto; 13, 14. Wessel Evertsen, skipper; 15. Asser Levy; 16. David Jochemszen.

BLOCK O

1. Adolph Pietersen; 2. Jan Cornelissen van Hooren. The three small sheds were probably fishermen's sheds; 3. Sybrant Jansen de Galma; 4. "The Hall in back of the Stadt Huys," possibly a storehouse; 5. Stadt Huys (City Hall), converted to City Tavern in 1653; 6. Rem Jansen; 7. Sybout Claessen; 8. Hendrick Jansen van der Vin; 9. Cornelis Melyn.

BLOCK P

1, 2. Charles Bridges, an Englishman, known as Carel van Brugge; 3, 4. house and tavern of Solomon La Chair; 5, 6. Charles Bridges; 7. tavern of George Wolsey; 8. Richard Smith; 9. Evert Duyckingh; 10, 11. Abraham Martens Clock; 12, 13. Richard Smith.

BLOCK Q

1, 2. the stillhouse and smithy of Burger Jorissen; 3. estate of Govert Loockermans; 4. Metje Juriaens; 5, 6, 7. Jacob Hendricksen Varravanger; 8. tavern of Andries Rees; 9. Ide Cornelissen van Vorst; 10. Immetje Dircks, widow of Frans Claessen; 11. a double house owned by Teuntje Straetmans and her husband Gabriel Carpesy; 12. Albert Cornelissen Wantenaar; 13. Pieter Jansen Trinbolt, "the Norman"; 14. Pieter Andriessen; 15. Jacob Jansen Moesman; 16. Arien Dircksen; 17. Abraham de la Noy, the younger; 18. Lambert Huybertsen Mol; 19. Trijntje Scheerenburgh; 20. tavern of Sergeant Daniel Litschoe; 21. Jacob Jansen Flodder; 22. John Lawrence; 23. Andries Jochemsen, occupied by Agatha van der Donck; 24. Andries Jochemsen, occupied by Claes Claessen Smith; 25. tavern of Andries Jochemsen; 26. Willem Pietersen; 27, 28. Goovert Loockermans, merchant, house was later owned by the famous pirate Captain William Kidd (1691–95); 29. Johannes van Brugh; 30. Burger Jorissen.

BLOCK R

1. tobacco warehouse of Albert Andriessen; 2. Hendrick Egbertsen; 3. Hendrick van Bommel; 4, 5. Willem Cornelis; 6. tavern of Pierre Pia, a Frenchman, owned by Joh. Verveelen; 7. Jan Jansen Hagenaar; 8. Andries Claessen; 9. Claes van Elslant; 10. Albert Andriessen.

BEYOND THE WALL

1. Sybout Claessen; 2. Jacques Pryn; 3. Lysbet Tyssen, widow of Maryn Adriaensen.

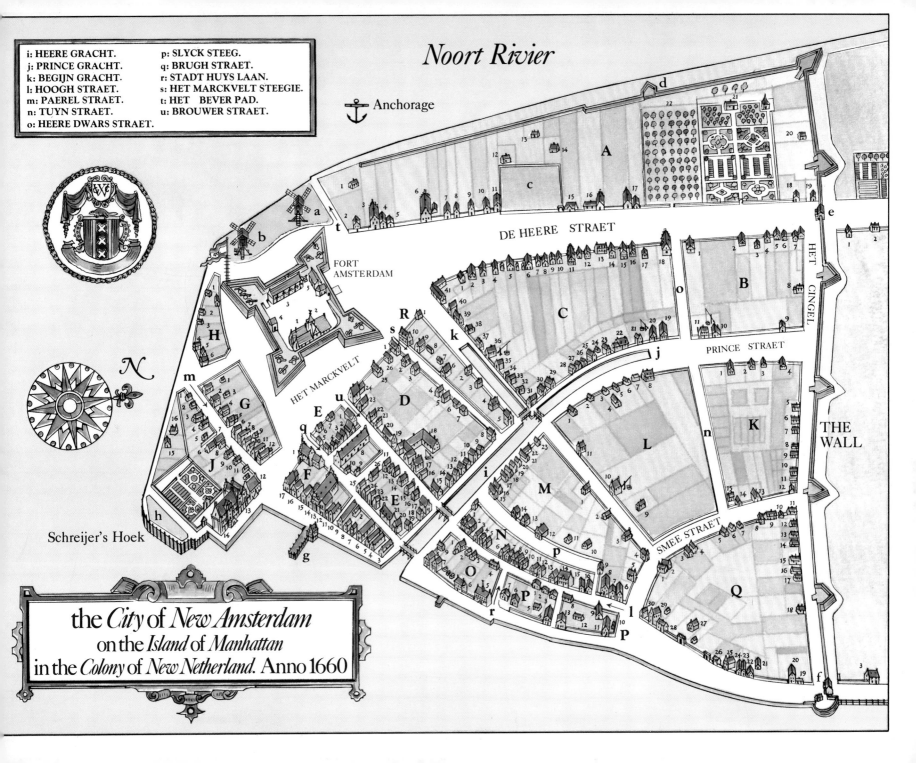

Noort Rivier

i: HEERE GRACHT.
j: PRINCE GRACHT.
k: BEGIJN GRACHT.
l: HOOGH STRAET.
m: PAEREL STRAET.
n: TUYN STRAET.
o: HEERE DWARS STRAET.

p: SLYCK STEEG.
q: BRUGH STRAET.
r: STADT HUYS LAAN.
s: HET MARCKVELT STEEGIE.
t: HET BEVER PAD.
u: BROUWER STRAET.

Anchorage

DE HEERE STRAET

FORT AMSTERDAM

HET MARCKVELT

HET CINGEL

THE WALL

PRINCE STRAET

SMEE STRAET

Schreijer's Hoek

the *City* of *New Amsterdam*
on the *Island* of *Manhattan*
in the *Colony* of *New Netherland*. Anno 1660